Unlocking Potential

Q
QUESTIONS
PUBLISHING
COMPANY

Unlocking Potential

How ICT can support children
with special needs

Sally McKeown

The Questions Publishing Company Ltd
Birmingham
MM

First published in 2000 by
The Questions Publishing Company Ltd
27 Frederick Street, Birmingham B1 3HH

© 2000 Sally McKeown

Cover and text design by Al Stewart

ISBN: 1-84190-041-9

Contents

Using *Kid Glove*, a keyboard accessory designed to help
visually impaired pupils

Preface

IN THE summer of 1999, I started to write a series of articles for *Special Children* magazine to give some background to the then new New Opportunities Fund (NOF) Training. My brief was to provide an overview of the technology available and explain how it could be used to support children who were statemented.

The special needs categories were taken from the Code of Practice:

- dyslexia;
- physical disability;
- speech and language disorders;
- visual impairment;
- hearing loss;
- communications;
- emotional and behavioural difficulties.

In addition there was an introductory article about NOF funding, the use of electronic communications and the role of British Education Communication and Technology agency (BECTa), the government-funded agency responsible for the National Grid for Learning and the Virtual Teachers Centre.

The series, which ran from September 1999 to June 2000, gave a clear overview of what was available for staff to use with each category of special needs. It was well received but, as with all articles about technology, quickly became out-of-date. This book is an attempt to collate all that information, update the software, and provide a few sample case studies to show the technology in action in *real* classrooms.

Acknowledgements

Thanks are due to my colleagues at BECTa: Chris Stevens, Mick Thomas, Terry Waller, and Maureen Quigley and her team who have provided case studies and checked software. I would also like to thank Inclusive Technology who have supplied illustrations for their own, and many other companies' software, as well as the following organisations for software samples and pictures: CENMAC; The ACE Centres; Semerc; TAG and Widgit.

Introduction

IN THE 'information age', technology is moving forward at a mind-boggling pace. People can now do things with computers that would have been considered science fiction as little as five years ago. The sophistication of the technology can often lead us to believe that it could be an answer to all our prayers.

However, this is unlikely to be the case with education and particularly with the education of learners with special educational needs (SEN). Technology can only work when it meets the needs of the learner and of the curriculum.

No matter how powerful the technology, integrating it into teaching will only work if:

- it helps to meet the learning objectives;

- both teachers and pupils are confident about using it;

- pupils have frequent and appropriate access to suitable technology;

- use is established across all areas of the curriculum, and newly learnt skills can be applied in other contexts.

This book looks at a number of areas of SEN, and shows how Information and Communication Technology (ICT) can contribute to teaching and learning. The information and examples are of a practical nature, and will be of use to classroom teachers across all age ranges and settings. They will also be of use to teacher trainers, advisers and inspectors who wish to disseminate good practice in the use of ICT.

The information should be used to initiate discussion within schools and to enable individual teachers to develop new and innovative ways of using technology. It will be particularly helpful to those who have undertaken training in the use of ICT in the curriculum, currently being funded by NOF. Those who have reached the required standards in this training will find plenty of suggestions for new software and its applications.

Technology in the classroom should not be seen as a new and separate initiative, to be implemented in isolation. It should be seen as an integral part of teaching, learning and managing, which makes all these tasks easier and more effective. In his report 'Information and Communication Technology in UK schools' (March 1997), Dennis Stephenson, the Prime Minister's personal adviser on ICT and education, claimed that ICT should:

"Serve education in particular by helping students to learn more effectively and by helping teachers to do their professional job."

We hope that this book will contribute towards implementing that vision.

Chapter 1
Lightening the load

No one goes into teaching because of a passion for administration, but every year the proportion of paperwork increases. Up until now, teachers have been filling in forms (often by hand) and sending them to the school office to be word-processed. Far too much time is wasted in education, in which the same pieces of data are being processed in many different offices.

Of course, many of these tasks could be simplified by using standard Word templates or databases, preferably standardised by the Local Education Authority (LEA). The Government has set a target that, by 2002, "administrative communications between education bodies, the Government and its agencies will cease to be paper-based". We are going to have to address the issue of record keeping and transfer information about pupils between schools, LEAs and the DfEE.

All teachers and school librarians are expected to be computer literate by 2002. Although this seems a tall order, NOF has provided 230 million pounds for training staff. Special Educational Needs Coordinators (SENCOs) will need to ensure that they are clear about their training needs, so that the school's NOF allocation is spent wisely and the SENCOs get the training most relevant to them.

Code of Practice
ICT can make recording and reporting a less painful process. Record keeping is a key component of the Code of Practice and one that is often very time-consuming. ICT can support SENCOs in developing, modifying and tracking pupils' Individual Education Plans (IEPs). Schools will keep records to ensure that:

1

- individual pupil's needs and appropriate strategies for meeting those needs are identified;

- all parties – specialist services, LEAs, teachers and pupils themselves – are fully informed of their role in supporting that pupil;

- appropriate resources are identified and planned for.

Some LEAs have created simple word-processor templates for collecting data, and small commercial companies and individuals working in schools have created their own databases. More recently, programs supporting the development and management of IEPs have become widely available. These usually contain statement banks that catalogue achievement criteria, resources, class strategies and support needs. The statement banks can easily be altered and added to, so that they reflect the particular needs of a pupil.

IEP Developer is particularly interesting, in that it provides a child-friendly IEP card as a working document for teachers and pupils alike. This program focuses on the secondary market and is designed to reduce bureaucracy. All the reports fit onto one sheet and cover basic skills targets, as well as personal and social development strategies. It is important to note that this program is most successful when used as part of a whole-school initiative, in which senior management involves all the staff. In this way, pupils' progress is monitored across a range of lessons and not just by the SENCO.

There are many other programs that are equally effective. These range from simple statement banks on a disk, costing under £50, through standardised databases for recording and reporting (from around £150) to sophisticated management information systems, costing over £1,000, plus annual maintenance costs. The choice has to be that which suits schools' needs best.

Email and Forum

Under the National Grid for Learning (NGfL) programme, all schools can expect to be connected to the Grid by 2002. Once this is implemented, most teachers will be online and will be able to communicate with busy educational psychologists or SEN support services via e-mail. Hopefully, this will improve the flow of information within local authorities. However, teachers also need access to expertise and opinions *outside* the LEA. They need to share information and advice with other teachers in similar situations.

The BECTa home page

SENCO-Forum, managed by BECTa, was started in 1995, to support SENCOs in their work. It provides a unique 'electronic meeting place' between practitioners, specialists and academics, where information and comments can be exchanged. Topics have included subjects as diverse as assessment issues, curriculum entitlement, parent partnership, inclusion versus integration, the operation of support services and arrangements for transition from special to mainstream school, as well as queries about particular syndromes and their educational implications.

The Forum has gone a long way towards meeting teachers' needs, and offers a convenient way of keeping in touch. "I like the speed of it all. I post a query and there may be two or three responses by the end of the day," reported one SENCO. Others value the practical support. "You get real up-to-the-minute information on SENCO-Forum because it comes from people who are directly working in the field." The national perspective is also valued. "It is easy to get parochial and think that our way of doing things is the only way. But then you get someone else's perspective and you think, 'that's good - we could do that here'."

On courses, delegates always value the contact with others in their situation and the Forum provides a virtual conference. "I am the sole SEN 'expert' in the school and I often feel quite isolated. I am supposed to know everything but I have few opportunities to network, discuss issues or update my professional skills. SENCO-Forum gave me a 'community' of like-minded people, who were willing and able to provide mutual support."

The Forum has grown considerably since its inception and there is a danger that it could become unwieldy as more people choose to take part. It could, in theory, become yet another administrative chore, although this does not yet seem to be the case. Membership now approaches 1,000, and the recent number of messages has varied between 200 and 400 per month. The large number of participants does not seem to have driven people away. It appears that, as teachers become used to the medium, they use practical strategies to cope with the deluge of e-mails, just as they would with printed materials.

SENCOs have found that the advice, information and practical suggestions they receive from other members saves them time, encourages them to try out new approaches, and provides quick solutions. At the very least, they are reassured to know that they are not alone – if they are struggling with things, others are too.

In the classroom

Teachers often want to find out about enabling technology, and make decisions about its usefulness, before buying it. Using the web they can see samples, download trial versions or contact companies to ask questions.

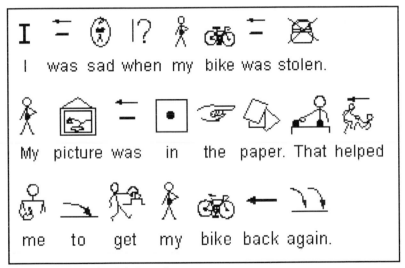

An example of Widgit software

When deciding whether to use information technology, it is useful to first establish what it will be used for, and question whether it might be better to use a simple, non-technological approach. Consider what you want to do, plus any problems pupils may have, then see if ICT can help. Often, labels such as 'dyslexia', 'learning difficulty' or 'visual impairment' are unhelpful. You need to pinpoint the problem more accurately. Some people with dyslexia may experience major problems with reading, sequencing and distinguishing left from right; others may have problems with particular aspects of writing or spelling. Sometimes, learners make progress when given access to a keyboard, because they can see all the letters and select the ones they need, instead of having to visualise and write each one in turn.

Similarly, some children find it easier to read from a screen than from paper, because the screen is lit from behind, and different colour combinations of text and background are possible. A CD-ROM with a speech facility can support and encourage reading or provide information for someone who is unable to read. Technology can raise motivation and can occasionally work miracles with intractable pupils.

NOF training

In March 1999 schools received a letter and a large red folder containing details of the NOF training scheme and its expected outcomes. A range of paper-based material to help teachers identify their training needs was available on request.

CD-ROMs from the Teacher Training Agency (TTA) have also been sent to all schools. These contain case study examples of the effective use of technology in primary and secondary classrooms. Their strength lies in the fact that they show real teachers using a range of equipment, plus the thinking behind each approach. You are shown lesson plans, specific pieces of apparatus, and an analysis of the lessons. While working through the materials, you can create an onscreen profile of training priorities, so that you are using the technology actively from the start.

The CD-ROM includes eight filmed case studies with comments and analysis from both the teacher and the TTA. Although the case studies show software and hardware being used for pupils with particular special

Key features for training in ICT have been identified to help teachers and school librarians to achieve the expected outcomes of this scheme:

● *a focus on the knowledge, understanding and skills teachers need to enable them to make decisions about the effective use of ICT in the classroom;*

● *integration of training in IT skills with training in the use of ICT in their subject;*

● *most training to be provided through school-based learning, involving the use of ICT in the classroom;*

● *a close link to the development of the National Grid for Learning and to the National Literacy and National Numeracy Strategies;*

● *at the end of their training, all teachers will be helped to develop an action plan for their future development in the use of ICT.*

(From the NOF web site http://www.nof.org.uk/educ_frame.htm)

needs, in most cases teachers will be able to generalise and apply the information to their own situation.

There is a grant of approximately £500 (per serving teacher) to be spent by schools on training courses approved by NOF. The NOF training will ensure that teachers are able to communicate electronically with other teachers and schools to share good practice. Nevertheless, there are concerns about how relevant the training will be to SEN staff.

The NOF documentation states that: "Teachers of pupils with special educational needs will be able to undertake training in their specialist areas. While there will be some differentiation built into the examples for curriculum subjects, staff whose pupils have 'severe and complex' needs will need something extra." It is important that SENCOs are critical users of the system if they are to obtain the best results. They need to pinpoint exactly what sort of training staff might need, and ensure that their provider can satisfy these requirements.

As a result of bidding processes, there is now a small group of providers offering training in this area. In many cases, specialist organisations have joined forces to form consortia. The Special Needs Learning Network, led by Semerc, is focusing on learning difficulties across the board, including special schools. There are four main modules:

- *Access to the Curriculum* will help children get to grips with science, humanities or the other key areas;

- *Communication* covers sound, symbol, text and graphics;

- A multimedia option;

- *Higher Order Skills for Teachers* includes using the web, improving productivity and making materials.

The training will be delivered through a combination of CD and Web resources. There will also be software samples, so teachers can try out different products and find out what best suits their circumstances. Two key elements of training will be the online e-mail mentoring, and the case studies, which contain examples of real classroom practice. Teachers will build a portfolio by choosing a route through the modules, working through a range of case studies and completing a number of set tasks.

The Deafchild UK Consortium includes the following organisations among its partners:

- The Deafax Trust;

- British Association of Teachers of the Deaf (BATOD);

- The Royal School for the Deaf in Derby;

- British Telecom.

This consortium proposes to train 450 teachers of the deaf over two years. Teachers of the deaf need to find out how to use ICT to support the core subjects of English, mathematics and science. They need training so that they can compare the relative merits of ICT with other teaching approaches.

Inclusive Technology is the only SEN provider working in all four countries in the United Kingdom. It is also the only organisation concentrating on learners with profound difficulties. Its consortium has the impressive title Inclusive Consultancy and Training Syndicate, and includes a host of specialist partners including the ACE Centre North, CENMAC and the Advisory Unit, all of whom have expertise in communication difficulties. In Scotland there is the CALL Centre, SCET and Edinburgh University. Other partners include the Down's Syndrome Association and the Royal National Institute for the Blind. Manchester's Metropolitan University is validating the units of training and is responsible for quality assurance.

Intellitools

Although much of the training will be delivered via e-mail and web-based conferencing, there will also be a more personal touch. Schools will get a two-day consultancy with a technology expert who also has experience in supporting young disabled people in schools.

The following site provides good sources of SEN expertise:

Useful websites

To join SENCO-Forum send an e-mail to majordomo @ngfl.gov.uk with the following message: subscribe senco-forum.

The archived messages can be viewed on the Web at: http:/ /forum.ngfl.gov.uk/senco-forum/

Some other useful sites are listed below.

http://www.inclusive.co.uk
Practical advice to people with any interest in special needs and ICT, including articles and details of support organisations that offer more general assistance regarding special needs.

www.nof.org.uk/educ_frame.htm

http://www.canterbury.ac.uk/xplanatory/xplan.htm
The *xplanatory* is a website maintained by the Centre for Educational Research, based in the Faculty of Education, Canterbury Christ Church University College. It contains pages of resources, information and ideas related to the support of learners with special educational needs.

http://www.granadalearning.com/special_needs
The Semerc information service contains a range of information on special educational needs, with a particular focus on ICT.

http://www.becta.org.uk/inclusion/index.html

The SEN section contains links to disability organisations as well as information on the use of ICT to support and include learners.

Official and government websites

http://www.ngfl.gov.uk/ngfl/index.html
The schools section of the NGfL contains a link to the Standards site, information for governors and parents, plus a link to the Virtual Teachers Centres in England, Northern Ireland, Scotland and Wales.

http://www.dfee.gov.uk/sen/senhome.htm
The DfEE's official website brings together information for teachers, governors and LEAs. It also contains some sample IEPs.

http://www.yearofreading.org.uk
The Year of Reading aims to encourage everyone to read for pleasure and for information. This site includes resources, advice sheets, news, information on events, plus a link to the Literacy Trust.

http://www.nof.org.uk/educ_frame.htm
ICT Training for Teachers and School Librarians (full details online).

http://www.teach-tta.gov.uk/index.htm
This is the Teacher Training Agency site. This gives details of the Needs Identification Materials to support the NOF-funded ICT training programme. You can find the expected outcomes here and also order the CD-ROM materials (which are free).

Using the Web

Once you have the skills, will there be high quality information for you to use? Anyone who has browsed the Internet knows that there is a lot of useless information out there. It may seem that the Web is a collection of junk mail, which search engines cannot always sift through. Search terms may throw up American sites and, while it is interesting to compare practice, it can be time-consuming and is not always relevant.

In order to address this problem, BECTa is working with the Department for Education and Employment (DfEE) to develop a new Inclusion site on the Virtual Teachers' Centre (VTC) which has been designed for learners, and for those teaching and supporting them. Inclusion is a free Gateway site (i.e. a site that has no content of its own but allows access to other sites more quickly). At the moment many of the resources have a disability and schools' focus, but the plan is to extend the content, so that it will look at broader inclusion issues.

This site presents an opportunity for resource providers, e.g. publishers, voluntary agencies, schools and service providers, plus anyone else searching for good materials to collect. BECTa will be inviting *anyone* with useful resources to catalogue them on this site and encouraging users to become actively involved in reviewing them and suggesting additions.

The world of ICT is developing rapidly and teachers need to change their 'mind set', so that instead of seeing ICT as another burden, they view it as a more effective way of working. If used well, ICT will *save* time as teachers use it for administrative purposes, for recording and reporting and for extending the range of materials available for use in the classroom.

Chapter 2
Physical access

WHEN PEOPLE think of physically disabled pupils, they tend to think of children in wheelchairs and those who have problems with mobility. They may be more concerned about ramps, toilets and access to the building, than access to the curriculum. In fact, there are many children who can walk but have physical disabilities that make it hard for them to communicate, keep up with work and engage in the same physical activities as their peers. Children with cerebral palsy may have poor speech articulation, which makes it hard for teachers and classmates to understand what they are saying. A ramp will be of little help here, and schools will need to think carefully about what access *really* means.

Effective communication is the key to successful integration. No child or adult can be at ease if he or she feels isolated and excluded from what is going on. While certain areas of the curriculum may be too physically demanding for such children, there should always be an alternative method of participating and contributing.

How can ICT help?
Computers can make all the difference. For pupils who struggle to form letters, who tire easily or have limited motor control, computers may be the only way of getting their thoughts onto paper. Teachers who participated in BECTa's laptop project found that word processing worked well for children with motor co-ordination difficulties, as they found it easier to press keys than form letters. They also found the keyboard useful for children with arthritis, and as a means of improving accuracy for children with poor fine motor control.

One teacher commented: "I have a child with poor fine-motor control and using the keyboard is helping him gain confidence," while another said: "A pupil in my class with arthritis finds it a real bonus."

In some cases, a desktop computer might be the best choice, because it has relatively big keys, a separate mouse and is quite robust. On the other hand, if a pupil is in a wheelchair, or needs access to a computer in different settings, a laptop might be better. The Panasonic *Toughbook* from Centerprise is a popular choice, because it can be attached to a wheelchair and is designed to withstand lots of bumps and knocks.

However, for a pupil who is walking and has to carry books and kit around a school, weight may be an issue. In that case, you may wish to opt for something like *AlphaSmart* or *Dream Writer.* These are cheap, have normal size keyboards with word-processing software and built-in scrollable display. Text is easily uploaded on to a Macintosh computer or PC for formatting and printing.

Using *Alphasmart*

Once you have a machine, consider how users are going to navigate around the screen. Most of us use a mouse, but this can be a barrier for some people. There are many options and alternatives that form part of the standard Windows environment and can improve access for physically disabled learners. These include slowing the mouse speed down, or using the 'sticky keys' option so that you don't need to hold two keys down simultaneously to carry out a command, but can press them one after the other. Another common problem is that users who have a tremor can end up with strings of unwanted letters. The filter key setting in the Accessibility option in Windows stops the letters from repeating themselves. These little adaptations may be all that are required for some learners, but others may need a little more support.

To find out how to adapt the Windows programme to make it more accessible for people with disabilities, try the following:

1. Click on the Start button in the bottom left-hand corner of the screen. Point to Settings, click on Control Panel, and then double-click on Accessibility Options.

2. Under Keyboard, you will find Filter Keys, which tell the operating system to ignore brief or repeated keystrokes.

3. 'Sticky keys' enable the user to use Shift, Control, Alt by pressing one key at a time instead of all of them together.

4. Under the Mouse option you can select keys which let you operate the mouse by using the numeric keypad.

5. In Windows and Windows 95 Control Panel there is a mouse icon. Here you will be able to change the speed of the mouse; adjust the amount of time needed for 'double-clicking', and swap the buttons over for left-handed use.

Mouse alternatives

Touch pads, joysticks and tracker balls are the most common alternatives to a mouse. As long as they can be connected in the same way as a standard mouse, they should work without any additional adjustment, other than alteration of the mouse speed settings in the control panel. Some users find that they are able to move the mouse, but cannot manage to control the buttons. A mouse interface, such as the *Mouser* available from Semerc, will allow the mouse buttons to be switched off and replaced by external switches if required.

Head mouse

The pointer on the screen can be controlled via the movement of the head. The 'head mouse' is operated by a small silver circle, which can be placed anywhere on the body, but is usually placed on the forehead. A sensor box is then able to track any movement. I recently saw a boy with a broken arm operating one of these. He had learned the technique very quickly and was able to play a game in a matter of minutes. It worked well in this case, because the pupil was confident, and not dependent on this form of access all the time. Ultimately, the student must feel comfortable with the technology.

The Tracker Ball

A tracker ball is a mouse that has been turned upside down. Instead of rolling the ball by dragging the mouse around, you move the ball only, using your fingertips. This means the device is stationary, and does not require much dexterity. *Kids Ball* is a large tracker ball, which can be used alongside any other mouse device. It's big and bold and ideal for young children or users who have difficulty using the standard mouse. Single keys can be programmed to operate as a double-click, or to simulate holding down

16

a mouse button to drag the pointer across the screen.

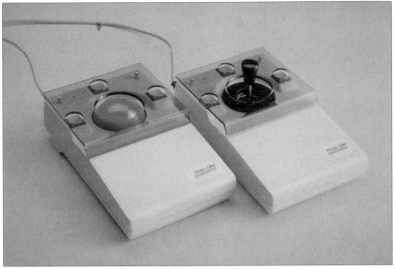

Trackerball and joystick controls

The joystick

For many people with disabilities, the joystick is a familiar device. It is found on most electric wheelchairs and has been a familiar feature of many computer games over the last decade. For some users this gives it a head start over other devices, as they will already have had considerable experience of using it in other contexts.

The touchpad

Touchpads are often incorporated into the design of the latest portable computers. They usually consist of a small pad that is operated by the touch of a finger. They will respond to the lightest of touch, and can be good for people with restricted movement. Some larger touchpads have an elevated stand for use on a desk, tray or tabletop. The smaller touchpads can be used in the palm of the hand and can provide an excellent alternative to a mouse. Not all children cope well with this device, however. One teacher reported: "A child with cerebral palsy in my class has to use a separate mouse, but he selects with the buttons under the glide pad."

Connecting it all up

In the past, one of the problems in using IT was connecting alternative devices to the computer. What happened when pupils had different needs but were using the same machine? The teacher had to switch off, load a new device and switch on again, maybe to find that it hadn't worked. This could often waste a great deal of valuable lesson time.

Nowadays, most new machines have a universal serial bus (USB) port on the back, and many devices are USB friendly. The advantage of this is that you can have up to 128 devices plugged into one computer, and the connections are quite sturdy with no pins that may get damaged. Best of all, the software automatically recognises the device when you plug it in, so you don't have to restart the computer.

Keyboards

Keyboard shortcuts make it easier to carry out many computer functions. For example: Control S saves files, while Control C copies a highlighted passage. There are hundreds of shortcuts, and users can also create their own for actions or sequences they might otherwise find difficult. It *is* possible to find your way around a programme without a mouse or similar device.

But what if the keyboard itself is a barrier? *Big Keys* is a chunky keyboard, which is highly robust and has a choice of either 'ABC' or 'QWERTY' layout. *Little Fingers* from Semerc is a small keyboard with built in tracker ball and wrist rest. It is ideal for users with limited hand movement. *Trackboard* is a compact keyboard, 30% smaller than the standard model, also with a built in tracker ball.

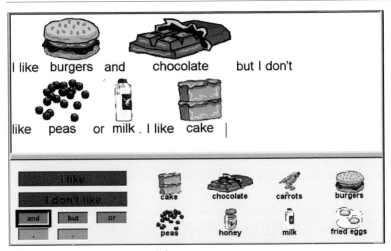

Clicker – an onscreen grid

Concept keyboards used to be very popular, but in recent years have been discarded in favour of on-screen grids such as *Clicker*. It is a pity that this is the case as concept keyboards are versatile tools, which teachers are once more beginning to find useful for navigating around CD-ROMs. Overlay keyboards, e.g. *IntelliKeys*, can also be used to control the screen pointer and the overlays come as part of a pack. It is quite easy to make your own overlays, to support specific curriculum activities. There is now an *Intellitools Activity Exchange* so that staff can try out other people's lessons, games and exercises. Some of these are from the USA, but British teachers and advisers are preparing an increasing number.

Switch control

For those pupils unable to use a conventional keyboard, special software utilities can allow single and double switches to access standard software. For example, by scanning across a grid, letters and words can be inserted into a word processor. New utilities are being developed which will provide switch access to a wide range of modern programmes, so that the switch user is not limited to the more 'traditional' activity of word processing. Software such as *Clickit* and *Hotspot* can give switch users quick, easy access to point- and-click software by defining 'hotspots' on the screen, which can be reached with switch presses. This is especially useful for switch users who wish to work with CD-ROMs.

Switch Access to Windows (SAW) can be used to give access to mainstream software. It is often used to help create hotspots on CD-ROMs, but can also be used in other ways, for example, one university student has set up a SAW template to help her edit videos for a media course.

Children using switch presses

Don Johnston Software's *Discover: Kenx* is a keyboard and mouse for students with disabilities. There are on-screen grids with lots of access facilities. The software controls the mouse so that the pointer moves around a grid, and rotates and tracks slowly in different directions. The *Discover* range is a complete system, which contains everything you need for physical access. As it is a complete model, there is no need to buy and add extra features at a later stage.

Text input

Some children find it difficult to put text together, and because they write slowly, they lose track of their ideas. First of all look at the Autotext facility, which you will find in the Tools menu of Word, under AutoCorrect. This handy device means that you can set up a list of abbreviations, which the computer will recognise and expand into words or even sentences. For example, if you are studying *A Midsummer Night's Dream*, you can save over twenty keystrokes by keying in *MSND* and letting the computer type it out in full.

Next, consider using word lists. If there are standard terms, for example, science words or vocabulary for a topic on the Egyptians, you can use *Clicker* or other onscreen grids.

One of the most frustrating things for physically disabled writers is that the whole process can be so slow. If children can only manage a few keystrokes per minute, it becomes physically exhausting, and ideas disappear before they can be recorded. An ideal solution is to type in the first letter of the word that you want and choose from the suggested words which then appear on the screen. If the word you wish to use appears, you press a number to select it. If it doesn't, then you type the next letter for a further list, and so on. The more often you choose a word, the higher on the list it appears, so the programme quickly learns core vocabulary for any subject. There are many good predictive packages to choose from, including *Co:Writer, Prophet* and *Penfriend.*

Even better for some pupils is *WordAid,* which is less sophisticated than some of the fully-fledged packages, but does offer topic word lists, as well as alphabetical ones.

Voice recognition technology seems an ideal concept for people who can speak but who lack good motor control.

When the user speaks, the words appear on screen. For this to work effectively it is necessary to have a fast computer, a good microphone and time to invest in the enrolment process.

Students found many advantages to using this system. Some with physical disabilities found that they tired less easily. Others were delighted with the sheer volume of work they produced, and staff commented on increased self-esteem. However, some users with physical problems found the system frustrating. It was sometimes difficult to cope with the physical effort of speaking loudly enough for the microphone to pick up.

A possible solution to this problem would be to invest in a microphone volume booster. This is a small box, which runs between the microphone and the machine, and boosts the volume. It is useful for laptops and, possibly, for some desktop machines.

There are currently two types of speech recognition software on the market: *Discrete* and *Continuous*. Mick Donnegan of the ACE Centre has found that the discrete systems may have advantages for learners with severe physical disabilities, such as dysarthria. One pupil, Charles, tried both types of speech software. Mick Donnegan reported: "With *Continuous*, he was not getting the immediate screen feed-back and he found the skill of dictation quite difficult. The time that it can take to edit in continuous speech can be prohibitive, also it is so much easier to miss your errors when reading back your work with continuous speech. With *Discrete*, he was able to feel more in control, he could correct errors as he went along, and see the errors he had made."

The text could also be read back using a product such as *Keystone*, an integrated programme that supports voice recognition packages and allows speech output. Many physically disabled learners start with discrete systems such

22

as *Dragon Dictate*, and become proficient in word-by-word dictation, whereas continuous systems such as *Via Voice* or *Naturally Speaking* require different skills. Some users liked the speed of continuous systems, whereas others found it harder to adapt to a different style of dictation.

While these facilities can improve access to standard packages such as word processors or spreadsheets, pupils need access to the curriculum too.

Access Maths is designed for children who find it difficult to use protractors or compasses for geometry. Using this, children can select the isosceles triangle tool, draw the base line, then click and drag, and a perfect example appears on screen. Similarly, with the polygon tool, a child can explore the properties of a range of shapes, including triangles, squares, octagons, and so on. (up to twelve-sided objects). *Access Maths* can also support primary school work on telling the time. It offers a clock tool, with analogue and digital clocks, which enables the child to learn about hours, minutes, seconds and 24-hour times. The teacher can then alter the programme according to the child's progress.

Access Maths is a maths processor. To use it effectively, pupils should have a firm understanding of the mathematical concepts involved, but the physical aspects of drawing and recording are made much easier for them. Interestingly, this programme is increasingly used to help children *without* physical disabilities because, like all good maths software, it represents an important step between abstract reasoning and the physical handling of materials. This aspect is one which children with physical disabilities often miss out on. They sometimes find maths particularly difficult to learn, especially in the early stages, when the practical experience of picking up toys, playing with water and drawing shapes is so important. Estimating skills often depend on physical contact, with plenty of walking, lifting, weighing and physical manipulation of objects.

Access Maths can also be used as a drawing tool. Most drawing packages rely on a click and drag approach, which is very difficult for some users. With *Access Maths*, children can draw lines, shapes, arcs and ellipses, and then edit them to change the scale or rotation.

Thurlow Park School in South London caters for pupils of all ages, with physical disabilities, and related language and communication problems. The school has won many awards for its artwork. Dave Nicholl, an art teacher at the school, has recently produced a book called *Pooling Ideas on Art and Imaging* (Trentham Books). He firmly believes that it is vital for all of us to be individually creative. Computers may help children who are physically incapable of being creative on paper. They might start with a scanned picture or a digitised photograph, import it into a paint package and use it as a starting point. "A good image manipulation programme is in some ways comparable to a good word processor. You can move fragments of an image round and expand or delete them. You can save your work in progress in stages, and keep several versions. The students become more experimental because they have the security of knowing that their work is safe. Many people whose ability to cope with the world in general is severely restricted are able to perform in a gifted way in the fields of music or art."

An example of one pupil's artwork, using an image manipulation program

Chapter 3
Sensory impairment

IN THE last chapter we looked at physical access issues. Here we are going to consider access to text, and ideas for those with sensory disabilities.

Access to text

Computers can provide alternative methods of inputting and accessing text. Within the standard Windows package there are many options that make it easier for visually impaired people to find their way around the screen.

Standard facilities

Brightness

It is often easier for some people to read from a screen than a book because there is light behind the text.

Colour combinations

Both the text and the background colour of the screen can be changed using the Accessibility option in Windows. Some combinations are easier to read for people with specific sight conditions.

Big print

It is easy to convert a document into large print. Some people follow text better if it is double-spaced. Alternatively, use the Zoom facility under the View menu in Word to increase the size of the text in the window. This does not affect the size of the text when printed out.

Choice of fonts

A font such as Helvetica or Arial may be easier to read on screen than a serif font (with feet at the base of the uprights) like Times, or a fixed-space font like Courier.

Sound effects

Many of us have warning sounds on our systems that bleep when we are about to close a document without saving it. There is a range of sounds available to alert blind users, when they maximise a window or open a menu. Look for these under the Sounds menu in the control panel settings.

The mouse pointer

In most cases, it is fairly easy to change the colour and size of a mouse pointer and to show 'mouse trails', which make it easier to spot where the mouse is.

Keyboards

How do we help visually impaired pupils to become competent users of technology? Initially, we need to ensure that they can find their way around the keyboard. As a first step, you might try putting large-print stickers on the keys. These come in several colour combinations. Alternatively, teachers may prefer to use a *Kid Glove*, a plastic keyboard sleeve with black letters on a yellow background. The advantage of this is that it can be lifted off when other pupils are using the keyboard.

In the longer term, both groups of users really need to develop touch-typing skills. Those with visual impairments cannot rely on their sight to correct mistakes. Hearing impaired pupils need to be able to watch a signer, to lip-read or pick up on non-verbal cues. Often, touch-typing tuition is organised on an individual basis, and staff may use a variety of materials, e.g. large print, taped or on-screen typing tutors. However, many of these are not designed for visually impaired learners and may not be suitable. Because most schools do not have a policy on touch-typing tuition (let alone tuition for a minority group), there is often a poor success rate for visually impaired learners. Programs should offer access through speech, and have a choice of font size and colour combinations. One good program is *Touch Type,* available from Semerc and Inclusive Technology, a straightforward typing tutor, in which the learner can see the letter, hear it and type it.

Type to Learn, from Iansyst, teaches students to type while reinforcing spelling, grammar, composition, and punctuation skills. *Touch-type: Read and Spell* is a computer programme based on the Alpha to Omega scheme. Originally hailed as a breakthrough for dyslexic learners, this package has many features, which make it useful for visually impaired pupils. It gives immediate feedback and a scoring system, which motivates children to keep trying. It has over 600 short modules; some students are able to manage ten modules in a session. A pilot project in Greenwich reported that visually impaired pupils showed a marked improvement in listening skills and spelling, as well as learning to be accurate typists.

Sound

Many learners with visual impairments rely on synthesised speech when using a computer. These programs read not only the text, but also the screen contents. Those with very severe difficulties may require specialised screen-reading software. A blind pupil can be made aware of what is on the screen by having all the information spoken by a synthetic voice. This might involve having each menu item, character or word read out, as you type. On computers with a sound and music facility, the speech output can be produced in a similar way through the main speakers.

On computers that do not have this facility, a separate piece of equipment may be required to make the computer 'talk'. There are specialist products that are tailor-made for the blind community such as *Jaws*. Alternatively, you might like to look at *Write:OutLoud* and

TextHelp, which offer a range of add-on facilities to be used alongside standard word-processing packages.

TextHelp

Alternatives to keyboards

IntelliKeys, a versatile overlay keyboard, is very popular with visually impaired users as it can be used with tactile overlays. It is useful for teaching Braille or Moon. With the companion program *IntelliPics*, you can create overlays for scanned books or other printed material. Students can sequence through the steps in a recipe, a story, or an experiment by pressing keys on their overlay. *IntelliPics* also has a quiz feature that enables you to turn any activity into an interactive quiz.

As new ideas and packs are being developed, they are being put up on an activity exchange on the website http://www.intellitools.com/. If you have *Intelllipics*, you can download and try out the activities. These vary from simple maths activities through to stories and software to help students in different areas of the National Curriculum.

Intellitools

Interactive whiteboards

The *Smartboard* is an interactive whiteboard that works in conjunction with a computer and projector. Some schools use these as a 'glorified' chalkboard but this is a very expensive option. The computer loads up software and then the board becomes active. Choose one of the four different-coloured pens and draw on the board, then wipe it clean with a 'magic eraser'. You can also use your finger as a mouse to drag pictures and other objects around the board.

In recent trials staff working with deaf and hearing-impaired pupils were highly impressed by the board, and felt that pupils would benefit from it. They considered it to be an excellent demonstration tool, since pupils did not have to listen to and interpret instructions, but could see what was happening instantaneously. One advantage of this is that everyone is looking the same way, whereas if children are writing or using a computer, they are looking down and may miss signing, body language or additional explanation. With the *Smartboard*, you are sure that they are looking at the right piece of information.

On the other hand, some staff found that in a classroom without blackout facilities it was not always easy to see the board. Also, the projector emits a beam, so the board may become obscured by shadows. Another potential problem is that as the board is lit up, it may detract from the speaker and make it harder for pupils to lip-read.

Acquiring language

There have recently been a number of CD-ROMs developed to support the acquisition of British Sign Language (BSL). These can help people who want to learn BSL in the same way that they might learn French or any other language. They can also help deaf children who are struggling to communicate in BSL. Another use, as with Manchester City College's new CD-ROM of maths signs, would be to help standardise the signs for particular concepts. This would save lecturers from having to create new signs. The college consulted experts who were not only knowledgeable about a particular curriculum area, but also were born deaf and had used BSL from very early childhood.

In this way, technology has become a means of extending and developing good practice and providing a permanent visual record of language, which can be used on a national basis.

Sign Now! is a different type of dictionary with over 3,500 signs (including some regional variations). You can access a sign by typing or clicking on a word, or by clicking on a hand shape. There is a quiz to try, or you can learn new signs by watching the relevant video clips. These can be slowed down or 'freeze framed'.

Sign It! from Sign Communique Ltd is the closest thing to a course on disk. It has over 200 video clips of conversations on topics students need to study for Stage 1 and Stage 2 BSL exams. As with the study of any language, learners need to move from single words, to phrases, to the creative use of language before becoming fluent, so BSL users need to be able to cope with conversations that are signed at a normal speed.

Sign It!

The Scottish Sensory Centre is releasing a CD-ROM for teenagers designed to keep them 'healthy, safe, sexy and sharp'. Designed for both deaf and visually impaired learners, the idea is to give them access to information that they might otherwise miss. The Royal Blind School in Scotland has provided voice-overs (working from Braille) for this, and Donaldson School has provided the signing. It covers issues such as contraception, safe sex and drug use, and is a bright visually attractive resource, which is a welcome addition to the area of Personal and Social Education (PSE). Also in Scotland, the National Deaf Children's Society has been awarded a substantial grant to run technology-based training events, launch a website and produce a CD-ROM of children's stories with text and signing.

Access to literacy

Phonological awareness (the link between symbol and sound) is crucial to literacy development, but how can children with a hearing loss access sound through visual means? In some cases, studying the shape of sounds on the lips might help, but lip-reading can be ambiguous. The words *white* and *quite*, for example, are virtually identical on the lips and are often deciphered by context. How do you teach children to break a word into syllables when they cannot hear it? The length of a word may not relate to the number of syllables: *beach* is monosyllabic, while *vid-e-o* has three beats, yet both words have five letters.

Some schools are using *An Eye for Spelling* from Teaching Handwriting Reading and Spelling Skills (THRASS) which focuses on word-level work and looks at the 44 sounds of the English language. Pupils learn how to break words down and see how they are made up of combinations of sounds, but they are working on a visual not an auditory pattern.

Fun with Texts can be used with any group, regardless of age, curriculum focus or language ability. Originally designed to teach foreign languages, including English as a Second Language, it is a framework program, which allows learners to interact with text. At one level it can be used to teach specific vocabulary and spellings: words appear on screen, then disappear, and the pupil has to type them in correctly. This is the basis of many spelling programs and is particularly good for checking and reinforcing half-remembered patterns. The advantage of using *Fun with Texts* is that the teacher controls the content. Alternatively, you might choose to create cloze passages where words are omitted and replaced by blanks. You can

32

also mix up lines of text and let pupils put them back into sequence. This is a good way of checking that pupils are reading for meaning. Once a child is completely familiar with a passage, perhaps from a well-loved story or from one of the Literacy Hour 'big books', you can choose the Prediction option. The package gives a choice of words (usually six), and you rebuild the text, bit-by-bit, by selecting the appropriate words. This helps to develop an awareness of syntax and sequence.

Another program for developing literacy is *Sign Graphics*, a My World program from Semerc. This enables teachers and pupils to create a *still* form of sign language, by selecting various parts of the body on-screen. Children can then begin to relate the language they use for day-to-day communication, to the written form on the page. All too often children learn to sign and then approach reading and writing in their second language. With *Sign Graphics* they can have access to books and to the wonderful world of stories. As they begin to enjoy reading in their first language, they gain confidence and become independent learners.

Sign Graphics

Using images

Unlike books, computers offer sound and images, which can supplement or replace the written word as a means of expression. Computer software can provide visual stimulation. There are a number of packages that display bright and attractive moving images. These can encourage children with visual impairments to make effective use of their vision and improve their tracking skills. Inclusive Technology's *Switch Suite* and *First Look: Patterns* images can be printed out for colouring in and cutting, to develop manipulative skills and hand-eye co-ordination.

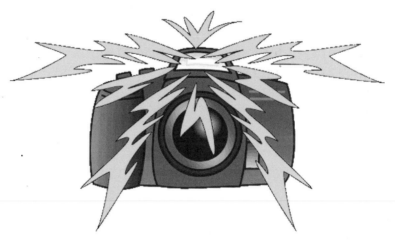

Gadgets

Pictures are important to deaf learners but, up until now, digital cameras have been expensive, and teachers have worried about giving them to children who may damage them. The 'Jam Cam' from TAG was short-listed for the Primary Hardware Award at the British Education and Training Technology show (BETT). This camera appeals to children in that it is bright yellow and easy-to-use. The prints are not of a high enough quality for glossy brochures, but are perfect for recording sports days and work in progress.

The use of digital cameras with PowerPoint is revolutionising classroom practice. Mike North, a teacher of the deaf, has been developing photo stories with the English department at the Royal School for the Deaf (RSD) Derby, and the pupils are using PowerPoint as a means of recording their experiences. Mike feels that photographs and pictures provide a good starting point for pupils with limited literacy skills. At one level they use pictures to practise sequencing activities, but then they move on to supplement these with text. ICT seems to provide the motivation for learners to persevere with written work in what may be their second language. As well as providing a stimulus for writing, ICT enables pupils to develop high quality output and to experiment with new techniques. They have also used PowerPoint files as a means of teaching, as teachers are able to create instruction guides using this versatile package. Why word process a document, print it and then have people read it while you are signing, or a pupil is trying to lip read? Using PowerPoint, everyone can see both the text *and* the teacher. You are also able to control which part of the text the pupils focus on, whereas on paper some pupils will always be reading a different paragraph.

Pupils using this package are currently working on developing an advertising campaign for their local town of Derby, with letterheads, information guides and brochures. With this technology, the children can create a draft copy and then modify and extend it to produce several versions for different audiences. This process helps to foster higher-level literacy skills.

Mike North has also used spreadsheets for 'modelling' with his pupils. They start with a topic such as the school sweet shop and look at children's eating habits. They then create a spreadsheet to show which products pupils are buying, how much they are spending and the calories they are consuming. The activity becomes more interesting when pupils start to look at the 'What if . . . ?' questions.

What if someone buys a Kit-Kat instead of a Mars Bar? Do they spend less and consume fewer calories? Mike finds that children respond well to the concept of modelling, and the fact that results can be produced in graph form (e.g. bar charts) helps them to understand the maths more easily.

'Have you bought your lottery ticket?' 'Not yet,' said Elizabeth.

Photostory

Multimedia

Hyperstudio from TAG is one example of a versatile multimedia program which can be used to combine resources, so you can have scrolling text for subtitles and video clips of signing, together with still pictures, text and sound. The BBC and TAG Developments have used this program to produce *Elmer,* the first Living Book created especially for deaf readers.

Each page of the book has three screens on the CD-ROM. One is for pictures, one for signing and one for text. The signing is provided by Lesley McGilp, who is well known for her work on the BBC programme *See Hear.* Like other multimedia books, the user can choose to hear the text.

The reader is a 16-year-old girl, chosen because she has a very clear voice, which will be easily heard by those with partial hearing.

From *Elmer*

Access to information

Most people get information from books, television or the media, but these sources are often inadequate for the deaf community or for people with substantial sight loss. When combined with additional software utilities, CD-ROMs and the Internet mean that these two groups can access information any time and anywhere in a format that works for them.

Information from the Internet arrives in a very compact form, and this can affect the pupil's ability to undertake independent research. According to Margaret Bennett, Chief Executive of the Library for the Blind, the *Oxford Child Encyclopaedia* has 57 volumes when it is translated into Braille. As a result, pupils tend only to look at the relevant volume, missing out on all the browsing and cross-referencing which is often the most rewarding part of research. With encyclopaedias on CD-ROM, it is easy to access information, which can then be read out loud by the computer.

Deaf children can learn a great deal from programs such as *My First Incredible Amazing Dictionary*, a skilfully designed package in which graphics and animation represent difficult-to-define words, or *The Way Things Work*, in which scientific concepts are explained by means of humorous cartoons.

Going online

These days there is often an assumption that ICT will be readily available and accessible to all. However, not all websites are suitable for non-sighted users. There are specialist web browsers available that can enlarge text and 'speak' the contents of a web page. This can be problematic, however, as a conventional screen reader reads text from left to right, across the page: if the text is in a magazine or column format, it will keep reading across from one story to the next, giving the reader a somewhat bizarre view of world events.

In January 1999, the BBC launched the BBC Education Text to Speech Internet Enhancer (BETSIE) which reorganises web pages into a more logical format, removing all the images and the unnecessary formatting, so that what you receive is the text content of the page. This makes it easier for screen readers to read the page to an online user. More details about BETSIE can be found at http://www.bbc.co.uk/education/betsie/.

Making friends

One of the best ways of using information technology is to help people keep in touch, not just with world events, but with one another. Writing and communicating should be an active process, and people talk and write better if they have a receptive audience and are given some feedback. Pupils with visual impairments are increasingly being integrated into mainstream schools, and while this is laudable for many reasons, it is equally important for them to have access to others with similar experiences.

In the VI (Visual Impairment) Resource base at Alderman Callow School in Coventry, an e-mail penpal scheme has been developed. Martin Bradbury, who is co-ordinating the project said: "The number of pupils we deal with at the resource base is small. We felt there was a sense of 'isolation' (being the only VI pupil around at times) which might be overcome by means of the Internet. Our pupils needed access to other VI pupils in different educational settings, in order to share experiences, information and frustrations. A pen-pal project seemed to provide the opportunity and context to meet these needs.

We drew up a set procedure for each of the aspects of using e-mail, so that a consistent 'path' was established, each time it was used. This meant that the pupils quickly became confident with the basic operations and sent emails right from their first lesson with this programme. It also meant that different members of staff were able to follow the same instructions for consolidation work, for example, at the after-school club on a Wednesday.

We are still in the early stages of sending and receiving e-mails. The National VI Athletics tournament is coming up in June and we would like to use that as an opportunity for some of the pen-pals to meet up. One of the pupils has already expressed an interest in contacting a friend who attends a different Coventry school, but who is on-line at home. Another pupil is due to move to a new school in September, so it is hoped that he will be able to keep in touch with us through the facility that exists at his new school."

Communicating at a distance

BECTa and British Telecom worked with Deaf@x to develop literacy skills in deaf children by partnering them with a hearing adult. The original project targeted seven schools and one college.

Staff reported improvements in grammar, drafting skills, syntax, punctuation and vocabulary. Social interaction became more important. Many were writing to an adult as an equal for the first time, using language to elicit and convey information. In many cases the children were exchanging personal information, and asking questions, instead of always trying to answer them.

Dear Zinat.
  I have a very bad throat and cough. I wear special glasses so could you write a bit bigger please.
  Where are you going to study and what are you studying?
I broke my glasses last week. On saturday my mum went to the shop to get me new glasses. They are pink,green,purple,orange and white. Do you wear glasses?
  from kelly xxxxxx

An example of work from the Deaf@x project

Now Deaf@x are working with children in India on a two-year programme to share good practice in the UK with teachers, parents and experts in the fields of literacy and communication. They will be linking up to demonstrate the use of telecommunications and the Internet to train deaf children. They ultimately hope to be able to improve literacy and communication skills in deaf children around the world.

When you reflect that, in the past, many young people with a sensory impairment rarely communicated with anyone who wasn't in the same room as them, you begin to appreciate the impact that technology has had on their lives. It has opened up a whole world of contacts and experiences.

Chapter 4
Language and literacy

LANGUAGE is highly prized in our society. Success and power are associated with good communication skills: the ability to speak, use language effectively and write in a clear and persuasive manner. As a society, while we admire those with physical prowess – footballers, for example – we do not respect them if they seem to be inarticulate. World leaders may not necessarily be those who *do* things, but those who *talk* about doing them.

People who are unable to talk clearly or articulately are disadvantaged in our society. More than half a million children have speech and language difficulties. Some of them have problems in producing the sounds. Children with cerebral palsy may be physically incapable of controlling their muscles sufficiently to articulate sounds, while other children may have lost the power of speech as a result of accidents or strokes. Autism affects 115,000 families in the UK. This complex condition disrupts the development of social skills and the ability to communicate. Autism affects four times as many boys as girls, and may be caused by biochemical imbalance or organic brain damage.

Whatever the cause of communication difficulties, the end result can be catastrophic with a child who is isolated, and whose every utterance has to be interpreted by a classroom assistant or a family member. Having no voice can mean not being able to express an opinion. In many cases, other people will finish children's sentences, speak on their behalf and decide what they will eat and wear. Not only are these children deprived of decision-making ability, but all too often, kind-hearted people pre-empt their opinions too: "Lisa likes music, don't you?"

Effective communication systems can break this cycle. The term Alternative Augmentative Communication (AAC) describes different ways that people with disabilities communicate with others. As the term suggests, these systems can be a replacement for speech, provide additional support to speed up the process, or make speech clearer. Some people use symbols, which could be drawings or photographs. There is *Makaton*, which has traditionally been used by those with learning difficulties, PCS (Picture Communication Symbols) from the USA and *Bliss*, which is a much more flexible system used by those with physical disabilities who are intellectually able.

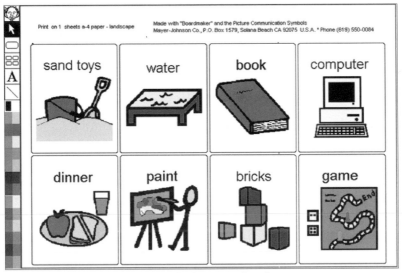

Picture communication symbols: *Boardmaker*

Electronic systems may seem to provide the perfect solution to this problem. Type in a message and it will be spoken by the computer, which will say exactly what you have written (swear words included!). In practice, however, this is not quite as simple. Users are limited by vocabulary sets, which give them functional language for school, but have little relevance to the demands of an active social life. Systems also break down, leaving the user literally 'speechless'.

Some children do not necessarily have a physical difficulty with speech. Some are very slow in learning to talk, while others cannot connect words in the right order to make a sentence. There are also children classed as having challenging behaviour, because they seem to say the wrong thing at the wrong time to the wrong person. These children never seem to learn useful non-verbal skills, or even the survival skill of when to be quiet. Sometimes they fail to follow verbal instructions or they misinterpret what is being said, causing frustration to their friends and family as well as distress to themselves. Children with these problems may frequently be labelled 'thick' because we tend to judge people by their verbal responses. If someone can't read but is verbally 'sharp' they may survive by developing good social relationships. Friendship is usually based on chat and social interaction. The silent child, or the child who has no effective language, is going to be isolated.

Children may have problems with the following areas of language.

Articulating sounds

Some children have speech problems such as a lisp, or an inability to pronounce the letter 'r'. While this is not life threatening, they may well be subject to teasing. Saying 'wabbit' instead of rabbit is typical of immature speech, and such problems are common: they appear in at least 10% of children younger than eight. Fortunately, these problems often disappear naturally as the child grows older, or can be overcome with speech therapy.

Receptive language

Some children who have no hearing loss still cannot gain meaning from speech. They hear the words, but the message does not come across. Some read very well, in the sense that they can decode the text, but may have poor receptive language skills. For example:

> Adult: "Dan put on his coat, scarf and gloves. Is it summer or winter?"

> Child: "Summer."

> Adult: "She went out into the dark street. Is it daytime or night?"

> Child: "Day."

People may accuse children of not listening, and quite often they are categorised as having some form of learning difficulty. Like some dyslexic learners, children who respond in this way may have problems hearing or forming rhymes, and may also be unable to identify sounds in words, or blend sounds together to make words.

Expressive language

Children with language impairments often have problems expressing themselves in speech. Some attach the wrong name to objects, while others speak in short stilted phrasing, or cannot answer simple questions. Some children seem to demonstrate similar characteristics to victims of a stroke or head injury. They may mix up syllables or the order of words in a sentence. Sometimes they cannot find the right word at all, or may substitute it for something quite bizarre. They tell stories in a random order without chronology, so that everything is jumbled and incoherent.

Parents and staff need to develop a range of strategies to encourage the child to speak freely in the way that is easiest for him or her. Learning to use sounds correctly can take a long time. With younger children, encouraging enjoyment of songs and nursery rhymes, and playing 'listening games' is good for language development. It is important to help the child to listen to speech and non-speech sounds, and to experiment with them, both in speaking and playing.

Talking books

Teachers have always used toys, books, and other materials as a stimulus for practising particular language skills, for example, learning to use the past tense or negatives. Computer software can be used in a similar way. The animation, graphics, and sound of many programmes make them lively and attention grabbing for children. Many children have a limited attention span and find the whole process of telling, or even listening to a story, difficult. Most of the talking books have lots of repetition that children can join in with, so that they are learning and practising different spoken language structures. Once they have heard the story, they can have a go at reading, and listen repeatedly to the parts that they have found difficult.

Wellington Square is based on the highly successful Thomas Nelson reading scheme and provides a very structured approach, not only to the acquisition of literacy skills but also to models of speech. The pupil is in control and can read and listen to the text, either word-by-word or sentence-by-sentence. There are also matching and sequencing activities which can be used to check and extend comprehension skills.

The Broderbund *Living Stories* are also widely available, and there are effective teaching materials to accompany them. The pupils can get involved in retelling the story, sequencing the events, naming objects and predicting what will happen next. Talking books provide a good context for language development.

One teacher found that the story *Ruff's Bone* worked particularly well with Paul, a seven-year-old who was unresponsive and avoided conversation. "For the first time he seemed quite animated and was willing to talk about what was happening on screen. It encouraged him to speak more. He joins in with the sound effects, listens to the text time and again, and reads along with it. It seems as if he has a reason for speaking now."

Another excellent set of talking books is *Rainbow Stories* from Resource. There are 18 stories, each read by a well-known person, including Julie Walters, June Whitfield and Gary Lineker. These stories take familiar nursery rhymes as their starting point and then introduce all sorts of twists to the plot. They also help with a range of concepts and grammatical forms, for example, 'big, bigger and biggest'.

So the three Bears, Mummy, Daddy and Baby went for a walk down the lane while the porridge cooled. Their tummies were really rumbly.

2

From *Rainbow Stories*

One school made excellent use of Sherston *Naughty Stories*. A group of children worked on *Toby the Troublesome Tractor*, and were asked to think about what might happen in the next story. They used a multimedia program with an Oak recorder (a software package which allows you to record from a microphone) and raided the Semerc *Treasure Chest* to find and use 'clip art'. Perhaps, surprisingly, they were all keen to talk into the microphone and had to think about what would be an appropriate tone of voice (which was quite a difficult skill). Using the Oak recorder with its visual display of sound waves helped some children to improve both the volume and intelligibility of their speech. The children then shared their story with the rest of the school.

Because their books were for a real audience, the children were motivated to check and self-correct their speech. They made far more effort with individual speech sounds because they had an incentive to get them right.

Using signs and symbols

One interesting new project involves teaching hearing children BSL. *Signs for Success*, a project in which seven schools in the Nechells area of Birmingham participated, has shown that the use of sign language with young hearing children can raise their English vocabulary levels by 20%. The project, which uses a CD-ROM called *Simple Signs*, works mainly because it is multisensory, and the links between signs and words make the memory work more effectively

Simple Signs

Hazel Atwell from St Clements School in Birmingham feels that signing has a lot to offer in terms of classroom management. "We use hands, arms and signals a lot in early years education as a way of reinforcing messages such as 'Hurry up!' or 'Sit down'. In a way, this project is just an extension of that. It is a great way of crossing the divides. We have children with special needs and also children who have little knowledge of English when they start school. Signing doesn't preclude anyone in the way spoken language can. Children on the fringes are brought in and signing can support emerging reading and language skills."

Symbol support can also be provided within other software. Widgit Software and Inclusive Technology Ltd have combined forces to develop *Inclusive Writer*. This program comes with many different literacy activities on CD, and you can also design your own. It could be used to set up an activity with an appropriate word or phrase bank – and then to get pupils working on sequencing activities, story starters, non-fiction writing and rhyming words.

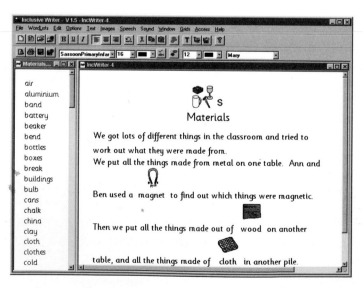

Supporting pupils' writing: *Inclusive Writer*

This program has over 2,500 coloured images and you can easily add your own. Most of the images come from the Mayer-Johnson PCS collection of symbols, supplemented by a selection of the Rebus symbols from Widgit Software. Line-drawing images arc also included. The picture support can be switched on and off, so that learners can select the words that they would like illustrated.

Talking word processors

Young children with emergent language or literacy skills can use talking word processors that contain a text-to-speech translation programme. When text or icons are typed in, the computer reads the entry. One such program, *Write OutLoud* by Don Johnston, also includes a talking spellchecker.

One feature of many talking word processors is a choice of synthesised voices, which will read out the words. You can allocate various voices to different parts of the text, thus creating dialogues and mini-plays with two or three characters speaking their parts in turn. While these programs cannot take the place of sophisticated communication systems, they have a range of uses, and can offer support, both to children with speech and language problems and dyslexic learners with poor sight or sound correlation.

Supporting dyslexic learners

Dyslexia is a specific learning difficulty, often noticed when an apparently intelligent child fails to make satisfactory progress in reading and writing. This condition is often linked with poor spelling, but in fact has many links with speech and language disorders. Dyslexic children often trip up when pronouncing words, and may omit or reverse syllables. They may also have problems with sequencing and ordering ideas, which means that issuing a list of instructions can be a recipe for disaster. If you ask a dyslexic child to do four things, one will almost certainly be left out.

The strategies and software ideas suggested earlier in this chapter will be relevant to a dyslexic child, but families and teachers will need to think carefully about what is needed as the child progresses through school. Talking books on CD-ROM may lead to taped books, and word lists of key vocabulary may be replaced by a predictive word processor.

Many people wonder if they might be dyslexic. There are several ways of getting an assessment, and you should contact the British Dyslexia Association (BDA), Dyslexia Institute or Adult Dyslexia Organisation for up-to-date information on local facilities. Schools now aim to identify children's strengths and weaknesses in order to find the best strategies for teaching them and to try and stop failure before it starts. CoP's *Baseline Assessment* is a piece of software designed to assess children when they enter school. Once staff are trained, it is quick and easy to use and produces reports that show a child's individual strengths and learning needs.

For older children try *Mastering Memory*. This is not an assessment or game, but a program based on the work of Buzan and Feuerstein, which teaches people a range of strategies to improve their auditory and visual memory. *Wordswork* is a new program from Iansyst, which has received considerable praise. Designed for secondary pupils and adult learners with dyslexia, it has an interactive approach to study skills, and covers essay writing, revision, handwriting and time-management.

Dyslexia and maths

'Seeing' and 'doing' are keywords for teaching mathematics to dyslexic pupils. It is important to minimise verbal explanations. If the learner is given a sequence of instructions before carrying out a task, he or she is doubly handicapped. Firstly, short-term memory may be lacking, so that one item may be omitted. Secondly, since sequencing is a problem, the child may get the instruction order wrong. Teachers should encourage dyslexic learners to see how numbers fit into patterns, rather than expect them to memorise number facts.

Estimating and checking are vital skills for dyslexic pupils, who may often expect to get a 'wrong' answer, and become discouraged. By estimating answers they can begin to take a measure of responsibility for their own work. Some learners find calculators useful, not just for getting answers 'right', but also for learning about products and number bonds.

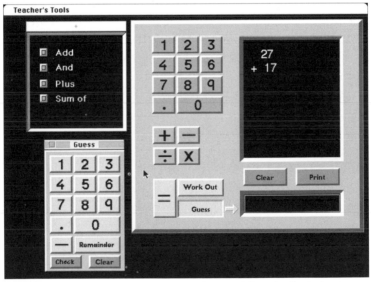

The *Interactive Calculator* is a useful tool for dyslexic learners

The *Interactive Calculator* from Inclusive Technology combines clear visual presentation, auditory feedback and physical manipulation to help dyslexic learners. Unlike other calculators, this one comes with a 'guess' button to encourage estimation. Dyslexics may find the following skills difficult:

- counting;
- visualising numbers;
- number concepts, e.g. what is a 5?
- notation and orientation of numbers;
- sequencing, does 35 come before 42?
- place value;
- symbols;
- number bonds;
- remembering times tables;
- shape recognition or naming;
- patterns.

Spreadsheets can also be a useful way of encouraging pupils to 'have a go' and experiment more confidently with numbers. Many students can perform the calculations necessary to solve a problem, but have difficulties in recording their work. Setting up a spreadsheet can encourage good habits in the layout of problems, which may transfer to work with pen and paper. Students can see a problem set out in front of them, and are therefore less likely to become lost in the process of calculation.

Getting text on the page

Dyslexic students often write so little that it can be hard to make any constructive comments, which is disheartening for both staff and students. Iansyst have a wonderful pen called the *Quicktionary Reading Pen*, which scans in written text and will read it out loud. This solves the problem of children having to copy out their work, which can be a time-consuming and pointless task for many learners, and often results in illegible, inaccurate text.

Writing consists of far more than putting correctly spelt words onto a page. It should have content, structure, and a proper framework. *Inspirations* is one of a new generation of planning tools which work on 'mind-mapping' principles to help dyslexic learners gather and develop ideas in a visual and productive way.

Draft:Builder is a new planning tool from Don Johnston, which has speech support and switch access. Pupils can start with the Outline option and write the headings. These can then be expanded in the Notes area (which can also be used by the teacher to create a writing frame). Next, the draft facility can be exported as a text file or turned into a cloze passage to reinforce spelling, vocabulary or syntax. This is an ideal planning tool, which will help pupils to overcome 'blank page' syndrome.

Another useful product is *Word Bar* from Crick software. This has a writing frame facility with phrases that characterise particular writing formats, e.g. formulating arguments or writing reports. These help give structure and cohesion to the writing. They can be edited and adapted by teachers, and can also be used as a memory prompt. Here is an example from *A Christmas Carol.*

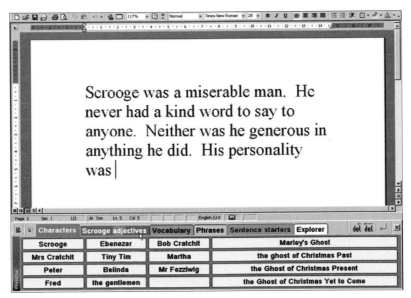

Word Bar: A Christmas Carol

Voice recognition

Voice input technology is now becoming popular and many UK teachers are currently trialling packages such as *Simply Speaking*, *Dragon Dictate* and *Voice Type* with dyslexic learners. So far, the reviews are fairly mixed. On the one hand, voice technology seems to work well when used by adults, in quiet environments such as the home or office, but there are other important issues for dyslexic learners. Some learners have major problems with enrolling the software. This generally involves the child having to read a large number of sentences to allow the software to match voice to text. Frequently, children cannot read the test sentences fluently, because the reading level is too high. To improve accuracy (particularly in the early stages), they will also need good proof reading skills, which may also be a difficult area for dyslexic learners.

Above all it is vital to keep things in perspective for dyslexic learners. It is too easy to fall into the 'deficit trap', and to see their work as a series of shortcomings. With the right ICT support, transcription is no longer an overwhelming problem, and teachers can begin to appreciate the syntax, vocabulary and sheer vitality of good writing.

The Accelerated Learning Centre at Stanbridge Earl's school has taken part in a recent DfEE-funded voice recognition project managed by BECTa. They have been investigating the use of this software with dyslexic pupils of secondary-school age. They used *Via Voice Executive* for this, but found that the original enrolment script was too difficult for their students. They were subsequently invited by IBM to write their own script, which has an approximate reading age of ten years.

"Above all, we've appreciated the pleasure it affords students and teachers to enjoy language and even to enjoy it when they make mistakes," said Edwina Cole, head of the Accelerated Learning Centre. " We've had such fun printing the recognition errors – so important when before, mistakes only produced tension and a sense of failure."

The Stanbridge Earl's school experience

● *The speech of the user is improved – becoming slower and more distinct.*

● *The students can think through their ideas – having control of the PC gives them the time and ability to structure their thoughts.*

● *The students can bullet-point their ideas.*

● *The system aids punctuation, almost without the students realising it.*

● *The system also encourages proof reading – which is much more convenient when done on screen, with corrections made by voice.*

● *The skill of following text with a cursor, and using the playback to spot errors, is important.*

● *Using the correction box encourages word recognition.*

● *Students have the freedom to use the vocabulary they would prefer, and not just the words they can spell.*

What about spellings?

Sometimes people confuse good literacy skills with accurate spelling. There are plenty of people who spell correctly, but are otherwise poor writers. Their work may not make sense, even though there are no spelling mistakes. Nevertheless, spelling ability is highly regarded in our society and computers can help in many ways. Some pupils have problems with reading and spelling which link very closely to their speech problems. For example, Joan could not say the 's' sound in front of many consonants so she would say and write 'kip' instead of 'skip'. Some programs such as *Starspell* allow the teacher to enter reading or spelling vocabulary, and these items can be related to the particular sounds or spelling structures that the pupil is working on.

Spell checking

All word processing systems now have built-in spell checkers. These are improving with each new version, and some can now recognise common dyslexic errors. The benefit of spell checkers is that they start with the vocabulary the pupil wants or needs to use, rather than a list of out-of-context words, which reinforce a rule. On newer versions of Microsoft Word, incorrect words are underlined and clicking the right mouse button brings up spelling suggestions. Some people argue that this is not educational, and that children should be learning to spell independently. There are two answers to this. Firstly, some children spend so much time on basic spelling that they accomplish little else and *still* fail. These tools give them additional help where they need it. Secondly, many people learn to spell as a result of using spell checkers, as they are repeatedly shown the correctly spelt versions of their chosen words. Spell checkers prevent children from altering already correct spellings (which is a common problem), and they offer an instant support that few teachers can match. They also allow learners to begin to take responsibility for their own spelling.

For those children who need spelling support on the move, and have reasonable phonic ability, Franklin *Spellmaster* is the ultimate in 'any-time/any-place' technology. This device can be used on field trips, in science labs or on a visit to a museum – in fact, all those places where a computer or a dictionary might be difficult to access.

The *AcceleRead, AcceleWrite* programme uses special cards

and a talking word processor. It is an excellent tool for learners in Key Stages 2 to 4, and is particularly useful for improving short-term memory, keyboard and spelling skills. The learner has to read a short sentence from a card, then remember it, repeat it and type it into a talking word processor. The learner then listens to the sentence and checks that it is the same as the original. The process is as follows:

- read;
- remember;
- repeat;
- type;
- listen;
- reflect.

After six hours' tuition, the first group to trial this program demonstrated a substantial improvement in their spelling skills, which was maintained over a full year.

Skill	Mean increase (months)
Word recognition	8.3
Spelling	4.1
Auditory short-term memory	15.3

(Results of Somerset Talking Word Processor Project)

This project, which used the *Talking Pendown* word processor, was very successful. Details of the scheme can be found on the Iansyst website. However, the teaching technique can be adapted for use with all children, and shorter sentences, either composed by the teacher, or taken from a reading book, can be used to good effect with younger children.

Students can make rapid progress using a spell check and speech facility together, in packages such as *Write OutLoud* and *Read & Write*. They can see the text appear on the screen, and then hear it read back to them. As a result, they begin to think in sentences and to plan ahead. Pupils can progress to write more coherently, at greater length, and become more ambitious in their choice of vocabulary.

Chapter 5
Access to experiences

IN VIEW of recent initiatives you could be forgiven for thinking that education is simply a matter of improving literacy and numeracy skills. However, part a school's role is also to broaden the mind and give pupils access to a wide range of experiences. In the past, many pupils with special needs had a very narrow curriculum and led quite restricted lives. They were usually collected from their homes and taken to school by bus.

On leaving school, many went to work in sheltered workshops and continued to live at home. Their social circles were restricted and their lives dominated by routine and familiarity. It was often assumed that they could not cope with change, and indeed many found it very difficult since they had experienced so little variety.

Nowadays, things are different. Adults with severe learning difficulties routinely go abroad. Some have even cycled around India to raise funds for charity. Pupils with emotional and behavioural difficulties undertake work placements and are able to record their experiences with digital cameras and multimedia presentations. Pupils who find mobility a problem can use virtual reality to explore historical ruins, or experience the delights of skiing. Sometimes the problem is not the range of experiences education can offer, but getting children to participate in them at school.

Out of school

The Audit Commission reports that 40,000 children per day play truant, 12,000 are permanently excluded and 150,000 are suspended for a given period of time. In June 1999, The Mental Health Foundation published a report entitled 'Bright Futures', promoting children and young people's mental health. The author, Helen Kay, claims that one child in five is likely to suffer from psychological problems before the age of 20.

There is no magic solution for dealing with the emotional or behavioural problems of a young person. However, ICT can provide a non-threatening environment to work within. The computer offers a neutral setting in which to experiment, so students feel confident and in control. Many learners with emotional and behavioural difficulties find it hard to relate well to other people and can find group-work, taking turns and being part of a class quite stressful. Using IT may help prevent discipline problems because teaching styles have to be adapted. Instead of being the 'authority figure' or 'expert' at the front of the class, the teacher becomes a guide and mentor, and the relationship becomes less confrontational. Teaching becomes more individualised with the accent on discussion and problem solving rather than passive listening.

Many football clubs are now running study centres to attract young people into education. Leicester City Football Club has provided sessions for 160 children a week, from 11 schools. Primary school children attend between 3.30 and 5.30 pm, and older pupils work there from 5.30 to 7.30 pm. The centre offers plenty of up-to-the-minute technology including digital cameras and interactive whiteboards. At present, literacy and numeracy are the core activities, but they will soon be using virtual reality to encourage pupils to learn French. The project is aimed at a range of pupils who need a boost with their education. Some are very able and need extra attention, while others need close supervision and have to learn to work in teams with other children.

The 'zapper' culture

As a result of the changes in popular culture, children now process information in a completely different way from previous generations. They are the so-called 'zapper generation', who have learned to assimilate numerous short pieces of information presented at high speed. ICT offers them a dynamic, professionally designed environment, with immediate access and fast results.

Adventure games often receive bad publicity, especially when they convey messages that contradict what we are trying to teach children. Children who play arcade games may easily jump to the following conclusions:

- that violence is perfectly acceptable – (if it moves kill it!);
- that 'bad guys' are always defeated;
- that death is reversible.

However, these messages are also present in cartoons like 'Tom and Jerry', so the solution is probably not to ban these games, but to discuss the issues involved and make sure that learners can and do distinguish between fantasy and reality.

However, computer games have much to offer children, if they are carefully selected. They can be highly motivating and, like other multimedia products, they are professionally made and have a high-quality image that is impossible for teachers to replicate. Games can encourage people to explore and try things out, instead of those people being passive consumers. They are also useful for improving skills of concentration, memory recall and hypothesis. The right sort of game can help people develop language skills and problem-solving strategies. Unlike textbooks, software can compete with television, and as people share solutions and ideas, they are also developing good communication skills.

This technology is the baseline for a generation brought up on Play Stations who like to enter different worlds and take on different roles. One product that effectively combines learning with an adventure game format is *Mission to Planet X*, part of the Internet Coach series. This takes users on a quest through 'cyberspace' where they learn about different functions of the Internet. The object of the adventure is to rescue Star Surfer from aliens. In the process of playing, children learn about surfing the net, downloading information, sending e-mail and safety issues concerning the Internet. This program features live actors, and excellent graphics, animations and sound. The good news is that you don't need an Internet connection, as Web simulations are used. The package comes with a set of lesson plans and worksheets relating to the National Curriculum.

Multimedia

The Alternative Education Centre in Jarrow has 53 Year 10 and 11 pupils, each of whom has been excluded twice from mainstream schools. The centre won an award for a CD-ROM that the pupils created using *Mediator*, a multimedia package with templates and professional design tools.

Christine Bell, head of the centre, said: "The pupils have been going to college and studying for the NVQ Level 1 in Multiskills Construction. This is the first time some of our pupils will get the full award. In the past they have always been good at the practical side but getting them to write down and record the evidence was like getting blood out of a stone. They produce text on a computer in a way they never would on paper. They use the tools, drag, drop and edit in a really professional manner. The technology has made all the difference."

These are the popular choices of the Perth Green pupils.

Painting and Decorating, Plumbing and Bricklaying

Pupils have used multimedia packages successfully to create their own CD-ROMs

Drama and role play

It is very important for pupils with emotional and behavioural difficulties to learn to get on with other people. There are programs available that deal with specific issues and might be useful for pupils who need to think about how they react to others. One example of this is the CD-ROM *Coping with Bullying*. In theory, every school in the UK (primary and secondary) should receive a free copy through their local Rotary Club, but there are still many schools that are unaware of this resource. This is the first of a projected series which will cover bereavement, racism, crime and coping with problems caused by divorce or separation. The *Coping with Bullying* CD-ROM will not be to everyone's taste, as at times the tone is a little patronising. Nevertheless, it does offer some sound advice on assertiveness, and suggests tactics to avoid becoming a victim of bullying.

Drama can also give learners a chance to experiment with different situations and roles. From TAG Developments there is *Stagecast Creator*, which enables pupils to create animated characters, invent rules of behaviour for them and make them interact with one another. The newest versions of *KidPix* allow users to create talking puppet shows, which might be suitable for younger pupils.

Another approach is using 'e-drama', which involves online role-playing. This might be effective for people who prefer anonymity, as well as those who like to create characters and take part in role-playing activities. Hi8us is a community organisation that works with young people to produce film, television, online materials and local exhibitions. They have been working with 14- to 17-year-olds in Pridmore, Coventry to produce a video and web materials. The e-drama developed from this project (http://www.hi8us.co.uk/home.html).

The Pridmore project

Graphics and symbols

Not so long ago, education for pupils with severe learning difficulties was limited to basic life skills such as shopping and cooking – indeed there is still a need for such courses. Nowadays, however, pupils with the same difficulties are learning French, using the Internet and processing digital images with an ease and confidence that many more academic people might envy. We focus far less these days on the concept of 'mental age' and concentrate instead on 'age-appropriate' materials.

These changes are partly the result of developments in technology. With the advent of Archimedes and Apple Macs, software has become more visual, and programs such as *My World* have shown the power of graphics as a tool for teaching and learning. Initially, the early versions were mainly aimed at primary-age children, with graphics to match, but soon programs were being developed for all ages, covering skills such as ordering a meal in French, planning a kitchen or designing a castle.

It was felt that with the PC domination of the educational market, software such as *My World* and symbol software such as the programs from Widgit Software would be unavailable, but this has not been the case. In fact, more sophisticated and powerful versions are now available. *My World 3* uses words and graphics, which can be supplemented with sound, animation and even video. *Writing with Symbols 2000* is a symbol processor that can be used in many different ways, e.g. for creating grids and importing photos and symbols. There is also an email add-on for this program, which is entirely visual and requires no intervention from teachers or carers. It can be set up so that there is a symbol or photo, instead of a name, in the address book. Children can write an email in words or symbols and then click on a picture of a bright red post box to send their message.

Learning languages

Symbol software and multimedia have also had an impact on the teaching of modern languages. George Hastwell School in Cumbria is well resourced in this area. "We started French in June a few years ago," said Clare Martin, Deputy Head of the school. "We began with a symbol library of French words. Since the pupils used the symbols for so much of their work, they quickly understood what the words meant, but getting them to read and talk in French was more of a problem. We used overlays with words and symbols so they only had to press three boxes to produce a sentence such as: 'Je voudrais du thé, s'il vous plait'. We also developed multimedia stacks with pictures of a café and a shopping scene, so they could click onto a picture and hear the word in French."

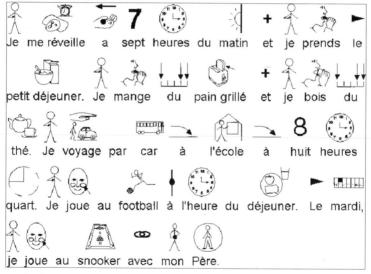

A symbol library of French words to support language learning

"We followed this up with a French week in school. We turned the sensory room into a French café with small tables, gingham tablecloths, empty wine bottles and candles (unlit!). The parents, governors and all the other children in the school were invited to use the café. For non-speakers, we provided an ORAC, a communication device where you press symbols to produce speech. ORAC proved to be a great breakthrough; it is less threatening than an adult and can be passed around the classroom more easily than a laptop. Even the Chairman of the Board of Governors used ORAC in the café, as he wasn't too confident about his pronunciation!"

West Oaks School, a generic special school in Boston Spa, puts great value on learning languages. They have been using *Project Presenter* to mix pictures and words, and French Clicker grids. Click on a picture with the left mouse button and you will hear a word, e.g. 'du fromage'. If you click with the right button, you will hear a request, e.g. 'Je voudrais du fromage s'il te plai'. Other grids are based on themes such as animals and travel. Sometimes, native French speakers are used, so that the children hear good models of speech. Pupils can add their own spoken vocabulary by using scanned pictures or photographs and recording their own voices, e.g. 'J'ai quatorze ans' or 'Ma chambre est petite'.

The school feels that links with other countries can bring languages to life. One group recently spent some time in Germany in a school near Cologne. The school used videophone to link up with its pupils while they were there, and their parents were able to come into the school to see this taking place. The pupils who stayed in the UK school used the Internet to find the host school's home page and sent emails to their friends, asking questions about the food and what everyone was doing.

Life skills

Some of the most interesting software is designed for adults but is also used increasingly by older pupils in school. *Lifeskills* is a CD-ROM developed by Inclusive Technology in conjunction with Knowsley Council and John Moore's University. It covers a day in the life of an adult with learning difficulties, and provides a framework for decision making at various levels. On one level it can be used for cause and effect. The user clicks and animations appear on the screen. The next level allows for identification and interaction as students are asked to find or choose certain things, for example they can help make a breakfast by choosing fruit and cereal. It also helps to foster curiosity as the user explores each scenario.

Life skills

This is one of the few pieces of software that has been designed for the older learner with profound and multiple disabilities, and access has been particularly well planned. It can be used with a single switch, two switches or with a touch screen. There is a wide range of support on offer, including Rebus symbols, Makaton and Signalong sign language. The settings are all depicted by black-and-white line drawings so that they are clear for those with visual impairments. One of the aims of this program is to give people an opportunity to take control. Often, people with multiple disabilities have little life experience and are given few opportunities for independent action and decision making.

Out and About is a CD-ROM designed to promote life skills for adults with severe learning difficulties. Designed by Home Farm Trust (a charity for learning-disabled adults), in conjunction with Semerc and Keele University, it covers the themes of shopping, travel, leisure, finance and going to college. All of the skills in this package fit in with the Oxford Cambridge and RSA examination board (OCR) National Skills Profile, and many aspects are linked to accreditation for Basic Skills at foundation level. In each of the five settings there are activities to help with perception and visual discrimination using exercises such as *Picture Matching* and *Spot the Difference*. There is also social sight vocabulary from everyday signs such as 'No entry', 'Pay here'. *Money Skills* and *How Many?* reinforce everyday numeracy skills, e.g. number recognition to 10, and working with money.

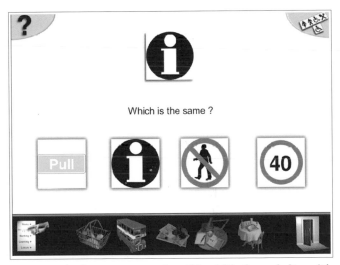

From *Out and About*: promoting life skills for adults with severe learning difficulties

These programs deal with life skills for adults with severe learning difficulties who are otherwise quite able, and can function independently with the right encouragement and support. The registration process of *Out and About* encourages independence from the start. Users have to key in their name, address, postcode, telephone number and date of birth. These are essential items of information which adults need to be able to provide on a regular basis. There is also the option of adding more detailed information, such as a National Insurance number, as well as an email address, as so many adults are now signed up with *Hotmail* or a college provider.

What to Wear and *What's Wrong* are sections on the CD-ROM that focus on decision making and learning about what is appropriate. All too often it is appearance and behaviour that single out learning-disabled adults from the other students in college. Instead of being street-wise and laid back they are sometimes noisy and may wear combinations of clothes that prevent them from blending in with the student population. *What's Wrong* tackles the area of social skills. Users watch a video and have to spot the social 'gaffes'. When they see inappropriate behaviour, e.g. eating your 'own' food in a restaurant, pestering other diners or shouting out for service, they click on the screen to take a picture of the incident. *What to Wear* takes them through the process of choosing clothing to suit the circumstances. This helps students to become more aware of the image they project, and may help those learners whose clothes are still selected by a parent or carer to become more assertive.

Music technology

Perhaps the most exciting current developments are in the use of creative tools for learners. Music technology allows pupils to experiment with, and make choices about, sound. Many people with emotional and behavioural difficulties may not have the patience or discipline to learn how to play a musical instrument, and the frustrations can far outweigh the delights. With recording equipment, they can record sounds and reuse them in different ways, or even record a number of their own performances and select the best ones. They then have the means to assess their performance, instead of being on the receiving end of judgement or criticism from others.

Rock and Roll your Own, from Mulltimax, is a versatile and reasonably priced resource. It contains eight pre-recorded songs, which are broken up into phrases. The user can then add sound and vocals from keyboard or microphone to create a 'sound collage', which can be recorded and saved. The program is designed for use by pupils at KS2 and 3 and contains very little text, but has been used and enjoyed by a range of people, including adults.

The Music Factory (PC), from Widgit Software, gives pupils the chance to explore sounds and build compositions at quite a simple level. They start by choosing a music genre, such as Blues, Reggae, Techno, or Salsa. They can select up to six instruments to include in the band, and each instrument has a number of musical patterns that can be sequenced or played live. The advantage of this is that the composition will always sound reasonable, however it is put together. It is also possible to create really satisfying music through careful listening and consideration of the different combinations. The Techno selection is particularly suitable for this, and has possibly the greatest appeal for this age group.

With Musical Instrument Digital Interface (MIDI) and sequencing equipment, pupils can experiment further still. They can edit sounds and create new compositions. By adding a keyboard it is possible to try out different tempos and accompaniments. Music technology represents part of the 'real world', outside the school gates. It also offers young people the opportunity to create something personal and meaningful for themselves.

Further information and resources

Software

Coping with Life (CD ROM)
PO Box 40
Ashington
NE63 8YR
Tel: 01670 813470
Coping with Bullying

MatchWare: Multimedia authoring software
Greyhound House
23 - 24 George Street
Richmond
Surrey
TW9 1HY
Tel: 020 8940 9700
Fax: 020 8332 2170
Website: www.matchware.net

Smile pack 8
Microsmile
Isaac Newton Centre
108A Lancaster Road
London
W11 1QS
Tel: 020 7598 4841

Touch-type Read and Spell
Computer Campus
PO Box 535
Bromley
Kent
BR1 2YF
Tel: 020 8464 1330

Write OutLoud (Co:Writer & Draft Builder)
Don Johnston Incorporated
18 Claverdon Court
Calver Road
Winwick Quay
Warrington
Cheshire
WA2 8QB
Tel: 01925 241642
Website: www.donjohnston.com

TextHelp
Lorien Systems
Enkalon Business Centre
25 Randalstown Road
Antrim, Co. Antrim
BT41 4LJ
Tel: 01849 428105
Fax: 01849 428574
(Or order from Semerc)

Touch Type
Semerc
Granada Television
Quay Street
Manchester
M60 9EA
Tel: 0161 827 2927
Fax: 0161 827 2966
Email: Semerc.sales@granadamedia.com
Website: www.semerc.com

Broderbund's Living Books
Mission to Planet X
The Academy of Reading – Autoskill
TAG Developments
125b Pelham Road
Gravesend

Kent
DA11 0HN
Tel: 01474 357350
Fax: 01474 537887
Website: www.tagdev.co.uk

Rainbow Stories Resource
51 High Street
Kegworth
Derbys.
DE74 2DA
Tel: 01509 672222

Inclusive Writer
Inclusive Technology
Saddleworth Business Centre
Delph
Oldham
OL3 5D
Tel: 01457 819790
Website: www.inclusive.co.uk

Home Mapper, Inspiration and *JamCam* available from
TAG
125b Pelham Road
Gravesend
Kent
DA11 0HN
Tel: 01474 537886

Writing With Symbols
Widget Software
102 Radford Road
Leamington Spa
CV31 1LF
Tel: 01926 885303

Clicker
Crick Computing
123 The Drive
Northampton
NN1 4SW
Tel: 0160 467 1691
Website: www.cricksoft.com

Wellington Square
Semerc
Granada Television
Quay Street
Manchester
M60 9EA
Tel: 0161 827 2927
Fax: 0161 827 2966
Website: www.semerc.com

PulseData International (UK) Ltd
(*Keysoft* software: scanners)
Blotts Barn
Brooks Road
Raunds
Northants
NN9 6NS
Tel: 01933 626000
Fax: 01933 626204
Website: www.pulsedata.co.nz

Wordshark
White Space Ltd.
Tel/fax: 020 8748 5927

Talking Pendown
Website: www.dyslexic.com

Sherston *Naughty Stories*
Sherston Software Ltd.
Angel House
Sherston
Malmesbury
Wilts
SN16 0LH
Tel: 01666 843200
Email: sales@sherstyon.co.uk

Castle Explorer
Dorling Kindersley
Website: www.dorlingkindersley.com

Starspell Fisher Marriott
58 Victoria Road
Woodbridge
Suffolk IP12 1EL
Tel: 01394 387050

Sign Now! available from
The Forest Bookshop
8 St John Street
Coleford
Gloucestershire
GL16 8AR
Tel (switchboard): 01594 833858
Tel (videophone): 01594 810637
Fax: 01594 833446
deafbooks@forestbook.com

Switch Suite and *First Looks – Patterns*
Inclusive Technology
Saddleworth Business Centre
Delph
Oldham
OL3 5DF
Tel: 01457 819790
Website: www.inclusive-technology.com

THRASS IT CD-ROM PC/MAC versions
THRASS (UK) Ltd
Unit 1-3 Tarvin Sands
Barrow Lane
Tarvin
Chester
CH2 3QS
Tel: 01829 741413
Fax: 01829 741419

An Eye for Spelling
LDA Ac/PC LDA
Duke Street
Wisbech
Cambs.
PE13 2AE
Tel: 01945 463441

ELMER (available from BBC Educational Publishing)
Freepost LS 2811
PO Box 234
Wetherby
West Yorkshire
LS23 6YY
Credit card hotline: 0990 210234

Sign Graphics available from Semerc

Learning how to Learn
(A CoPS popular assessment tool produced by Chris Singleton's dyslexia team in Hull).

Mastering Memory (Windows) software to help assess visual and auditory memory.
Only available from CALSC
Communication and Learning Skills Centre (CALSC)
131 Homefield Park
Sutton
Surrey
SM1 2DY
Tel: 020 8642 4663

Wordswork (Windows) A new study skills package available from Iansyst.
Iansyst Ltd
The White House
72 Fen Road
Cambridge
CB4 1UN
Tel: 01223 420101
Fax: 01223 426644
Website: www.dyslexic.com

Typing programs

1. *Type to Learn* (Windows/Mac.)
Teaches students to type while reinforcing spelling, grammar, composition, and punctuation skills. Available from Iansyst.

2. *Touch-type Read and Spell*
Specially designed for dyslexic learners by Phillip Alexandre.

3. *Touch Type* (Windows/Acorn/Mac)

4. *See, hear, type* from Inclusive Technology

Spelling programs

1. GAMZ *Player* (Windows) A CD-ROM containing all 28 SWAP/FIX games (from Inclusive Technology).

2. GAMZ *Word Search* (Windows) Generates word searches to improve spelling and vocabulary (from Inclusive Technology).

3. *Starspell 2001* (Windows) Look/cover/write/check plus human speech facility. Structured but has the option of including your own lists as well (from Fisher Marriott).
Fisher Marriott
8 Victoria Road
Woodbridge
Suffolk
IP12 1EL
Tel: 01394 387050

4. *An Eye for Spelling* (various versions). No speech facility, but a good program for a visual approach to spelling. Available from Rickett Educational Media.

5. *Wordshark* (Windows) 26 games for word recognition and spelling – particularly useful for Key Stages 1–3. Available from White Space.

6. *Units of Sound* (Windows) The reading and spelling program from the Dyslexia Institute. Available from LDA Multimedia.

Writing support

1. *AcceleRead, AcceleWrite* materials from the Somerset Talking Computer Project which can be used with any computer (published by Iansyst).

2. *KeySpell* (Windows) Additional spell-checking support that will 'say' the words, put them in context and work with voice recognition software. Available from:
Words Worldwide

9 Military Road
Heddon on the Wall
Northumdria
NE15 0BQ
Tel: 01661 854700

3. *Co-Writer* (Apple/PC) Designed as a word predictor for users with dyslexia or physical disabilities. Available from Don Johnston Incorporated.

4. *Penfriend* (Windows/Acorn) A prediction program to be . used alongside a word processor. The predicted words can be used with clicker grids. Design concept available from Inclusive.

5. *PredictAbility* (Windows/Acorn) A word prediction range of screen options, which learn the user's vocabulary.

6. *Prophet* (PC) Word prediction for Windows, providing speech and an intelligent word-ending feature. Available from the ACE centre.

7. *TextHelp* (PC) Provides word prediction alongside real-time, spell-checking speech, plus a screen magnification facility. Available from Iansyst.

8. *WordAid* (PC) Similar to predictors, except that it displays word lists in a fixed order, making it suitable for younger users. Available from the ACE centre.

Maths

1. *Interactive Calculator* (Windows/Mac) A multimedia interactive calculator based on research from Coventry University. (Inclusive Technology)

2. *Number Shark* (Windows) 30 games designed for learners with poor attention span, sequencing skills, and short-term memory. Available from White Space.

Hardware and peripherals

JamC@m from AlphaSmart 2000
(available from TAG Developments).

Alphavision Ltd
(suppliers of CCTVs)
North's Estate
Piddington
High Wycombe
Bucks
HP14 3BE
Tel: 01494 883838
Fax: 01494 881211
Website: www.alphavis.demon.co.uk

Dolphin Systems
(speech synthesisers and JAWS)
PO Box 83
Worcester
WR3 8TU
Tel: 01905 754577
Fax: 01905 754559

Dolphin manufactures a range of computer software, including screen-reading software, screen magnifiers and print scanning. Dolphin has multilingual speech synthesisers, useful for pupils learning French and German.

Kid Glove from Inclusive
Inclusive Technology
Saddleworth Business Centre
Delph
Oldham
OL3 5DF
Tel: 01457 819790
Website: www.inclusive-technology.com

Professional Vision Services Ltd
Philippa Wisbey
Wellbury House
90 Walsworth Road
Hitchin
Herts
SG4 9SY
Tel: 01462 420751
Fax: 01462 420185
Email: professionalvision@compuserve.com

PulseData International (UK) Ltd
(CCTVs, Keynote *Notetakers*
Mountbatten Brailler, Franklin Talking Dictionary)
Blotts Barn
Brooks Road
Raunds
Northants
NN9 6NS
Tel: 01933 626000
Fax: 01933 626204
Website: www.pulsedata.co.nz

Keyboard Stickers
Techno-vision Systems
76 Bunting Road Industrial Estate
Northampton.
Tel: 0164 79277

Speech Viewer III IBM
Tel: 0800 269545

Smartboards from Matrix Display Systems
Co-Writer Don Johnston Software
Don Johnston Incorporated
18 Claverdon Court
Calver Road
Winwick Quay
Warrington
Cheshire
WA2 8QB
Tel: 01925 241642
Website: www.donjohnston.com

Panasonic *Toughbook*
Centerprise International Limited
Hampshire International Business Park
Lime Tree Way
Chineham
Basingstoke
Hants RG24 8GQ
Tel: 01256 378005
Fax: 01256 322957
Website: www.centerprise.co.uk

DreamWriter
NTS Computer Systems (UK) Ltd
Aston Science Park
Love Lane
Birmingham
B7 4BK
Tel: 0800 731 7221
Website: www.nts.dreamwriter.com

Organisations

The Mental Health Foundation
20 – 21 Cornwall Terrace
London
NW1 4QL
Tel: 020 7535 7400

AbilityNet
Website: www.abilitynet.co.uk/fullvis/sponsors/features/
featfr1

RNIB
Website: www.rnib.org.uk

National Library for the Blind
Website: www.nlbuk.org

AFASIC
69-86 Old Street
London
EC1V 9HX
Tel: 020 7841 8900
Helpline: 0845 355 5577
Website: www.afasic.org.uk

NDCS
15 Dufferin Street
London EC1Y 8UR
Tel: 020 7250 0123

Scottish NDCS
c/o Veronica Ratray
293-295 Central Chambers
93 Hope Street
Glasgow G2 6LD
Tel: 0141 248 2429

Deafax Trust Technology Centre
Bulmershe Court
The University
Reading
RG6 1HY
Tel: 0118 926 0258

ACE Centre
92 Windmill Road
Headington
Oxford
OX3 7DR
Tel: 01865 759800
Fax: 01865 759810
Website: www.ace-centre.org.uk

Websites

www.stjohns.org.uk
A website by a school for the deaf – highly commended by
BECTa.

www.teletext.co.uk
A website providing a reliable source for news.

www.semerc.com
A website guide to special needs software.

Disability Net
Website: www.disabilitynet.co.uk/

A world-wide information and news service for all disabled people and people with an interest in disability issues.

Microsoft Accessibility
Website: www.microsoft.com/enable

Suppliers

Philip Alexandre
Tel: 020 8464 1330

Communication and Learning Skills Centre (CALSC)
Tel: 020 8642 4663

Don Johnston Incorporated
Tel: 01925 241642

Dyslexia Institute
Tel: 01784 463851

Franklin Electronic Publishers
Tel: 0800 328 5618

Granada Learning/Semerc
Tel: 0161 827 2887

Iansyst
Tel: 01223 420101

Inclusive Technology
Tel: 01457 819790

LDA
Tel: 01945 463441

REM (Rickett Educational Media)
Words Worldwide
Tel: 01458 254700

Official and government websites

1. www.ngfl.gov.uk/ngfl/index.html
The schools section of the NGfL contains a link to the Standards site, information for governors and parents, and links to the Virtual Teachers Centres in England, Northern Ireland, Scotland and Wales.

2. www.dfee.gov.uk/senhome.htm
The DfEE's official website brings together information for teachers, governors and LEAs. It also includes some sample IEPs.

3. www.yearofreading.org.uk
The Year of Reading (which finished in August 1999) aimed to encourage everyone to read for pleasure and for information. The site contains resources, advice sheets, news, information about events and a link to the Literacy Trust.

4. www.nof.org.uk/educ_frame.html
ICT training for teachers and school librarians. Full details online.

5. www.teach-tta.gov.uk/index.htm
The Teacher Training Agency website. This gives details of the Needs Identification Materials to support the NOF-funded ICT training programme. You can find the expected outcomes here and also order the CD-ROM materials (which are free).

References for Code of Practice and IEP software

Co-ordinator: Code of Practice Management
Kirklees School Effectiveness Service
The Deighton Centre
Huddersfield
HD2 1JP
Tel: 01484 225793
Email: marketing@geo2.poptel.org.uk

SENCO Capita Education Services Ltd
Stannard Way
Priory Business Park
Cardington
Bedford
MK44 3SG
tel: 01234 838080
Fax: 01234 838091
Website: www.capitaes.co.uk

SENCO Aid
Granada Learning
Semerc
Granada Television
Quay Street
Manchester
M60 9EA
Tel: 0161 827 2927
Fax: 0161 827 2966
Website: www.semerc.co.uk

IEP Developer
Special IT Solutions Ltd
PO Box 374
Cheltenham
Gloucs
GL53 7YU
Tel/Fax: 01242 254249
Email: enquiries@special-it-solutions.co.uk
Website: www.special-it-solutions.co.uk

IEPs software
SEN Store
HS Software
FREEPOST
Swansea
SA2 9ZZ.
Tel: 01792 204519 (24-hour answering service)
Email: h.s.soft@argonet.co.uk

IEP Writer
Learn How Publications
10 Townsend Avenue
London
N14 7HJ.
Tel: 020 8886 2262
Fax: 020 8441 1459
Email: learnhowpublications@btinternet.com